# THE UPSHOT

**Anne Rouse** was born in Washington DC and grew up in Virginia. After reading History at the University of London, she worked as a nurse and the director of a mental health charity. Since becoming a freelance writer, she has had many residencies, including visiting fellowships in Glasgow and in 2004-05 in Belfast. She lives in Hastings.

Anne Rouse has published four books with Bloodaxe, the collections *Sunset Grill* (1993) and *Timing* (1997) – both Poetry Book Society Recommendations – and *The School of Night* (2004); and *The Upshot: New & Selected Poems* (2008), which includes a new collection, *The Divided* (2008), plus a selection from her first three collections. She reads a half-hour selection of poems on *Poetry Quartets 9* (British Council/Bloodaxe Books, 2004).

# ANNE ROUSE

# THE UPSHOT
## NEW & SELECTED POEMS

# BLOODAXE BOOKS

ISBN: 978 1 85224 808 6

First published 2008 by
Bloodaxe Books Ltd,
Highgreen,
Tarset,
Northumberland NE48 1RP.

**www.bloodaxebooks.com**
For further information about Bloodaxe titles
please visit our website or write to
the above address for a catalogue.

Bloodaxe Books Ltd acknowledges
the financial assistance of
Arts Council England, North East.

Cover design: Neil Astley & Pamela Robertson-Pearce.

Printed in Great Britain by
Bell & Bain Limited, Glasgow, Scotland.

*For my mother,*
*Irene Munson Rouse*

# ACKNOWLEDGEMENTS

This book includes poems from three previous collections published by Bloodaxe Books, *Sunset Grill* (1993), *Timing* (1997) and *The School of Night* (2004), together with a new collection, *The Divided* (2008). 'Nude Descending a Stair' from *Sunset Grill* has been substantially revised. 'A Distance from the Sun' in *The Divided* is a re-working of part of 'A North London Planetary System' from *Sunset Grill*.

Acknowledgements are due to the editors of the following publications in which some of the new poems in *The Divided* first appeared: *The Dark Horse, New Welsh Review, Rising, Tall Lighthouse, The Times Literary Supplement* and *The Wolf*, as well as Tate Online.

I'm grateful to Julia Bird for her comments on an earlier version of *The Upshot*, and to John O'Donoghue for a conversation of many years. 'The Talk' is dedicated to him. A Royal Literary Fund Visiting Writing Fellowship at St Mary's College, Queen's University, Belfast, enabled me to write some of the newer poems. My thanks to both institutions, as well as to Bill Sillett and my family, for their extended support.

# CONTENTS

FROM **TIMING** (1997)

*upshot:* the last arrow in a tournament

# The Divided

(2008)

# Launderette

It'll all come out in the wash.
The blues turn mauve, the whites blush pink,
left to their whirligig and jostled fate.
Three coins, then enter the kingdom of the just,
and peer through soapy veils
into the steel belly of a gorgon; its routs
and reverses, the merely dross –
doubts, slights, the *he saids* and *she saids* –
sluiced right out. Then hoist the lot,
drenched second skins, into smoking sunlight.
Ah, but afterwards, they're back on your hands,
crackling with polyester guile,
reduced to the shapes you were, and are.

## Fool's Pardon

A scar of earth under a scant moon:
he'd walked the lough-side hundreds of times,
the man who'd taken down the town's flagpoles,
fussy with a dozen tired flags.

Shadows waited for him at the foreshore end;
it made page five in the city paper.
I asked fool's pardon of his living ghost,
having preceded him by daylight on that path.

Call that town of theirs a nether region, or his a case
of accident that hardened into merit
(ticking off the morning's task; his westward stroll),
I think we still could praise him.

'Fool's Pardon' is, I've been told by a Northern Irishman, a traditional term
for the licence given to the blundering or naive visitor.

# The Flag and the Maypole

A flag blusters from a maypole
in this crabbed town,
where twelve prosaic burgesses insist
on red-and-blue, and spurn the ancient green.

Away with flags of any stripe;
sandblast the mottoes off the city walls.
The white-wreathed, nuptial, boundless May
was never yours to sour.

Her single mission is to please.
What good can come of satyr squaddies,
khaki shepherds, dryads in camouflage?
O town councillor, get you with haste

under the greenwood tree
to sire, in riotous excess, your nemesis
and entwine this sorry relic, this maypole,
with purple loving ribands, in and out.

# The Discipline

*...detectives have arrested ten suspects but released them
after they refused to speak.*
(Associated Press, 10 March 2005) *

St Patrick's aftermath: the weekend bravos are roaring.
Green balloons rollick in a brawny wind.
In the May Street pub, it's quiet as a glade.
The TV mizzles; market traders dandle beer.
The dead's been barred; his havoc reels elsewhere.
Noon light sheers in through the blacked glass.

Next door, stalls flurry with handbags and soda bread.
A dog-eared elocution book (Dublin, 1859) reads:
'The Wolf is frequently referred to in Scripture.
Crafty and ferocious persons are compared to it.'
They washed the blood off their shoes under the tap here.
Silence turns a stolid face to this wall.

* Online despatch regarding the murder of Robert McCartney in Belfast on
30 January 2005.

# Lodgers in Southall

Up early, on Kabul time, a new guest
scans the brusque suburban lane.
His measured stillness burns
as if it fed on thinner air, on mountains.

One storey up, I'm about to fly this swallow's nest,
a narrow, lilac, servant's room
where pre-war Kentish housemaids scrawled
on tear-stained missives, *Hydrangeas, Southall.*

A thud; a swift kerfuffle overhead: a nervy scrum
of Bengali kitchen porters, rousted from
six hours' kip, rush one by one
to sluice round a vat in the bathtub,

scuffed and yellow, labelled, 'GHEE'.
Along the hall their glinting loafers parley.
My faux-hide carry-all is packed; I'm looking out,
one knee on the stripped bed, as last night's late

arrival ponders, his astrakhan blood-red against the slate-
and-tan of our pebble-dashed retreat.
Even before he turns, and I catch the ambiguous wonder
in his face, I hear, so this is England. *England.*

# Into Oak

By the morning they'd descended into earth,
their hats and shoes interned in rugged bark,
while toxins bled from them,
reddening to sticky buds,
and her murmur merged all sounds.

A traveller described them, halting in the bars:
their elderly, sparse ways; how he'd passed by
their farm at Advent, braved a streaming hill,
to find them twinned, and grieving into oak;
tall nettles guarding broken loom, and crook;

the hut riven into splinters as they'd creaked,
and burgeoned slowly, splitting earth, and sky.

# Childminding

Don't cry. The one who just undid you with a shout;
(who is ashamed, whose nerves are like catgut)
an alien voice, their baffling substitute,
one day will mean nothing:
will shrink to a razzing fly, half out of hearing.

Hush, small self, it's happened to those three,
the stay-at-home, the returnees lit with drink,
who whispered overhead, and blessed your sleep.
They were all so young, and thoroughly at sea,
it's likely you knew better, even then.

# The Waking

I've seen an oubliette in you,
a man-sized hole in stone.
The captive couldn't lie down in it;
the guards bet on his cries.

Enclosed in yours some time ago
for crimes against no one,
you've inched from it, hand over hand,
and overturned the grate

and fly tonight on a pair of ropes –
gossamer, that bridge across the moat.
It looks like mist from here.
I've scarcely breathed,

wishing you forward, sure-footed,
entwined with strands of spider's luck,
along hawsers, cross-ties,
and passageways, of sleep.

# The Talk

Diners light up the bistro windows.
Passing here by night you feel their liveliness,
a rush against the moorings;
along Villiers Street, a frieze of silent talk.

This alley off the Strand is no come-lately:
the raddled ghost of Kipling whistles 'Taps' upstairs.
Music hall soubrettes cadged cigs from here;
the Breton waiters took their bows each evening.

Over black olives and ciabatta, our talk is verve
in the glass, between leave-takings:
words at the barrier as times flash overhead,
then alert and alone, the iron rails gliding on.

Like two drinkers at Cana, our vintage deepens.
We repair to our separate coasts as the river's
trailing lights dwindle to a hum of motion,
the calm dark steadily enlarging there between us.

# The Wish

Walking along the Holloway Road, in the heat
and press of a normal Monday, I passed an alley
backed by a chain-link stretch of fence.

It was wavering, alive, the aluminium frets burst through
with hectic fronds; and I heard above the guttural traffic,
a keening, the *te deum* of starlings,

(a dozen stragglers from the local school)
and saw their object, out of reach,
motionless, negligibly small:

a tiny, neon-orange ball
in the drainage puddle's blackish mirror –
and think of it now, I guess,

because of some clamouring need
for the absent: for you, and your heartening word,
swiftly stooping; retrieved.

## After a Visit

Garbled, the gas flame frets
at the figure in the mirror across the room.
A tea-mug begins to stain;
the radio titters welcome.
Inland-green, smelling of salt,
voluptuous solitudes unfold.

My suitcase rolls into its niche.
House plants guzzle at the roots;
the fire nags about friends
mired while the other country floods.
*Thirty per cent of state troopers are in Iraq.*
*Everybody speeds. It's lawless.*

I saw one wreck, a light-blue sedan
wedged under a giant truck.
Fluorescent-yellow firemen,
motionless, and separate as trees,
watched their foreman place a hand
on the car door, and jerk it open.

# Landfall

Jumping ship, we tasted brackish waters.
The flame-red persimmon was strange to us,
the white dogwood. The chest of seeds, muskets,
and the King's Bible, we dragged above the tidal mark.
That winter we starved.

Happier to be a native prowling the stockade,
than John Poet, Esq, gnawing his own fingerbone,
or a wastrel's pockmarked daughter.
Homeward to you, to London,
unequal to the world we made.

Our players languished in that Roman stark domain,
obscuring Golden Virginia.
I scramble for the words you jettisoned
(preferring the Doric mode, and monied politesse)
Caliban burst from the wilderness.

The ship creaks windward,
small and dark and rank as an old shoe.
It rolls as the ocean rolls, wordlessly venturing
to where the words were born,
a forgotten card you sent yourself.

I'm scrofulous, emaciate, but I approach,
bellowing your open-hearted curses,
hard by the Isle of Dogs.

# Sign

That close-up of the body with the tattered foot,
slumped over the chain-link fence
in New Orleans; the sodden clothes and head-down
peeling skull, intimated how far he'd strayed,
as the black waters schlepped through gape and yard,
and cars rode belly-up. Tangled there, he'd stopped
like a runner at a stile, in the risen dark: half-vaulting,
yellowed, caught, in the back alleys of the kingdom;
sign for all eyes (v-sign or cross, or something like it);
up against the peremptory, the absolute hard.

## 99 Cent

*(photograph of a supermarket by Andreas Gursky)*


*This sordid plenty*, Updike wrote, but look:
the ceiling floats ensilvered, reds and yellows flirt,
the packets gleam, the jack–o–lanterns glare.
No lulling dark, no idle corners here.
Nothing could be more itself, candid and opaque.
The shoppers loiter, sidelined, muzzy wraiths,
and posters range across like sentries:
99c              99c              99c
presiding over the skein of shopping trolleys,
the paper towels, the juicy fruits, the mints;
the smothered cries of admen, some long dead,
*chuckles, hearts, tangoes, smuckers, grapehead*;
the Latin riffs and proverbs half-deployed:
*rolo, nutrageous, zagnut, almond joy.*

# Rubens' *St George*

A ruptured water main,
gravel jigging in its froth
like gnats, unsinking,
its runners gleefully flinging past,
brings Rubens' *St George* to mind:
the champagne charger's mane and tail,
ebullient, gusty spume.

Underfoot, and under-handed,
the dragon yawns like a drain,
blueish, uncompelling,
like the nearby drowned Leander,
rocked by sea-nymphs: mere foils for life,
for a brash courtier, rapt
over horses' hair, old men, and satin flags –

and *quidditas*, 'the whatness of a thing'.
The nereids dote on their drowned princeling.
Here's a coiling quickness, a cascade.
It pours, as watchers linger, caught
and eddied by the crowd
tracing the tendrils of the lamb's fleece;
a shadow on the hero's face.

# The Shadow

Under the esplanade is the last rough sketch:
a flat hat of stone; a darkened body of shingle.
A cardigan flaps – a mere appurtenance.
The tide stream flickers, and animates her.

The stones are her armoire, a three-piece suite
in green sateen, fringed with the wavelets
flurrying in, where the jetty's dissuaded
the breakers from the floor map of rocks.

She's had an intimation of what's to come;
the ridged cliffs tell of it;
grey and black, an *eminence grise*,
reduced by the sun and born each evening

into a series of irresolute shapes,
about to pay a smudged tribute to night
among the long shades, subsiding
until the silence can speak of her again.

# Rite

Sweltering giants hounded me.
One ambled close. *Here.*
I took the knife he offered, slick and cold.
*Write.* Pulling up his shirt,
he smirked, and dared.

His back was lightly freckled,
broad, and white.
I heard a furtive catching in his throat,
as the minute inscription ran,
and the shy blood spelled it out:
…N…and…O…

## The Verbals

Disliking even the word, *mistake*,
(the glass cobweb on the new specs,
vanishing French book, scabbed knee),
by thirty you'd digested another word, *foibles*.

Then, at mid-life, the word *failings* arrived
in the other's mouth. Cranky guard of a glass-house,
bluff, or rudeness – once you'd have thought, all this –
but oh my failings, what would I be without you?

Stuck in a fault; pinioned to a sky of stone.

## Small Thing

*(in memory of William Dashiell Rouse, Jr)*


Swollen with rain, the great cliff weighs
on bulkheads primed like heavy guns,
tilted across a littering of shells.
Free of salt accretions, stasis, a motor-boat
nudges towards the offing, attempting flight.

Memory husks, turns conjectural;
a man in a flak jacket, with prodigious Nikon,
back from the sea marshes, up with the dawn.
loping across the hotel corridor. I didn't see him,
my sister did, our sister, he passed us in an instant:

what you could have been. At seventeen,
you'd had a girl – desire, crimes, an epic – no small thing.
Even as an infant, bold at three, you'd tried
*en garde*-ing with a pen. I have the faint, blue tattoo still,
proud of the mark: a first word, left with me.

# Change

First she was a Sioux warrior, and then she was thirteen:
she sat in the grass like Miss Muffet, with an improving magazine;
brooded like an owl on a ladder, at the twilight's end;
wore a garter belt, let her hair grow, and the bloody cabaret ran
through the years like an Attic frieze, the oxcarts, the athletes, the pipes;
the rattling full cacophony parked in the sweaty nights –
all vanished. Her locus of seeds will be death seeds, that's her lot;
her purse of change, her blooms, narcissus, mandragora –
and her eyes in the mirror, are the eyes of twelve.

# Inland

Already the retiring light has inspected
the caterpillar train, clanking east to the apple;
the boys roping in the swan-shaped pedalos;
the fake palms and tea shacks; the hand-holding pairs
eying a stealthy white moon from the pier.

And still they sit, quiet; in coach-loads, in clans,
at tables tacky with spills; as sunburn frets
and the gulls adjourn inland; they drink, and sprawl,
peering out at the timeless, that great time
they are not having, but, somehow, will have had.

# A Distance from the Sun

After scarpering, fleet as winter lightning, from Nag's Head,
Venus and Mercury were apprehended –
(verbals judder through the squad car grille),
nabbed Rolex tucked amidships, when the pigeon's call
came in from Earth, an old girl selling fruit and veg at Seven Sisters.
All's right the this low world. Mars struts in his heaven –
he's the local vigilante, one ruddy, yawping blur as he enforces
some unofficial order's every clause.
Next, a drive to Madame Jupiter's for a round-up, or down;
J maudlin and rococo in a bisque dressing-gown;
a blue-jawed punter, Saturn, meekly schtum for all
his sweat-shop loot; an alert-breasted poster in the entrance hall,
the Titaness presiding, as their light-tempered foreman.

...The air miasmic with bribes; an impromptu doorman,
one Neptune, just off a tanker at Portsmouth, hapless git,
lisps and hovers, his wants shrunk to an infallible kit:
whenever the girl Uranus, self-cutter, strays, he'll follow,
adrift in the further radiant of sorrow.
We release him home, his uphill walk too stiff for pity,
where the gulls winter down the estuary.
Outside, swearing on the pavement, no job complete,
our lost blasphemer, Pluto. Rookies take his foul-mouthed bait,
then we're stuck all night in the lock-up – cries,
tears, bog's bottom. Peace, my son: he'll wander to the roundabout
or slink, invisible, into the frozen station.
If Hermes Whisperer repeats the world, to what does he return?

# Greensleeves

She held us, laughing, by the lychgate
(fetching in golden roses and Queen Anne's Lace),
with how, last night, she'd led a pilgrim crowd
to the charred sea-hut by the harbour wall
where the trulls sit, waiting for mainsails – and so we fear
her heart's contracted, that once was the lantern kind.

These wandering fits have taken her late in the day
(borne in by the upshot, the last arrow in the tournament,
the young priest says, of the lover who didn't stay).
It was long past sunrise, when she regained her empty bed.
My lady Greensleeves. Cicadas drowse through the whitening leaves,
the carillon sounds, and the temple doves refrain.

# Petition from the Sybil

I lost them to Charybdis,
the lubbers – lovers they'd be
if they'd persisted,
were stronger swimmers.

I blame myself.
I should have kept watch, shone
other than fitfully, as a landing light,
to cry out that a hidden shore was near.

The whirlpool smashed compasses,
coiled men in its murk,
stifled their pleas to the stars,
sucked them into the under realm

where the fish fled before them
and the sand rippled with thirst:
further they went, straight down,
Charybdis being the lure.

When I saw them again, years later,
on certain barges carrying coal,
or ships of timber, or in atolls,
in huts on stilts, hallooing drunkenly

to the clambering, tawny, young girls,
the spyglass spoke of lightless faces,
absorbed in a small relief:
a roll-up; a town gazette, months old.

It was my remorse for this, for these losses,
that drew me here to the court of Priam,
dead though he is. Let me reclaim
one former warrior; send him again to me

and I'll wrest him from his nightmares
of your goriest battle: of his own hand raised,
and the knife in it, descending,
and the other's terror, that called to his.

Let me take that man,
and I'll heal him with the sweeter toil
of diving, and mending nets on a shingle beach,
where the rocks have survived the oldest cruelty.

Give me this man, you Trojans,
who've known defeat.
You've outstripped your fortunes.
Let one amongst you, live.

# The Hive

Hoary with gold,
the bridesmaids gather.
Their flickering wings
fussily tend, and tend.

Finishing touches? No,
the waxen cells merely accrete,
like a chantry candle,
white and amber

while any prying hand
attracts a swift rejoinder,
a black imperial ball,
stiff retribution...

But the actual busy work of being,
the endless bringing to rights,
the work, the glorious damascene –
this does not end.

# Notes on a Metaphysic

Visually, a lyric poem is a map of its own genesis: a single thought surrounded by an empty field.

Consciousness has affinities with light and compression, while the material universe is usually seen as a dark expanse of outer space. The poem on the page appears as a photographic negative of the emergence of the consciousness into the material universe – a sudden introduction of the 'I' into whatever precedes it. We could call this the primary event.

Without consciousness there is no immediacy, no "now". A keen sense of the present moment animates the lyric poem, which relies on visual and thematic simplicity for its initial impact, while hinting at an underlying density of meaning. Through an engagement with poetic thought, linguistic invention, and image-making, consciousness intensifies within the force field of the poem – freed, for a moment, from contingency, while further committing itself to time and space as symbol and metaphor. While poems (or any art objects) 'make nothing happen' as Auden postulated, it's precisely their existence beyond the causal and the material, which allows the mind to move laterally. Any poem worthy of study will be guided to its ends, not by external demands, but by visionary promptings – that is, by the ever-evolving consciousness of writer and reader. 'Inspiration' is another word for this process of quickening, at the local level of the poem.

The spoken words of a poem arrive into silence. The word-sounds anchor the images in the speaker, and echo in the listener, through the affirmative, ritual action of voiced language. Poetry and dance have similar designs on their audience.

Both bring the preoccupations of what is usually called the collective unconscious into the physical realm. It's not much more of a leap, at this generalised level, to bring the collective unconscious into line with modern physics. Poets are fond of archetypes – 'the rag-and-bone shop of the heart', yet that other potent phrase of Yeats, 'where the ladders start' (the uncharted source of consciousness) may suggest an even more helpful hypothesis. Current research indicates that much of the universe is made up of an unexplained entity, and that there are serious discrepancies between quantum theory and relativity. These apparent anomalies are enough to suggest that, without resorting to supernatural explanations, we may inhabit two types of reality, or universe, in one. Consciousness may not simply be our window on the world, but a substantial, if immeasurable, part of it.

Speculative though they are, physical theories have implications for art and its practice. A metaphysic that centres on consciousness only highlights what poets already do. A contemporary poet, especially, will attempt to edit out of a given poem those elements, such as unnecessary verbiage, or glibness, which are antithetical to the mind's free working. However, this monitoring role potentially extends far beyond the page. By positing that 'the waste remains and kills' and 'getting and spending we lay waste our powers', William Empson and Wordsworth were identifying obstacles to the full play of consciousness, the inert and the trivial impeding individuals and societies alike.

Poetry makes itself happen, and although as good citizens poets assume other, necessary duties, their central task is to celebrate consciousness as it encounters the visible world. While the contemporary poem remains – for English speakers at least – a minority interest, poetry can claim a wider role through its collaboration with other genres, from film scripts to textual art, across culture as a whole. A perpetual foregrounding of language and the articulation of fresh perceptions, via the poetic, help to renew not only language, but all thinking and making.

Whether written in the spirit of defiance or in hope of communion, a true poem affirms the mind's free play, suggesting – perhaps at times predicting – a fairer, more vital world.

# The School of Night

(2004)

# Sighting

Old, smiling man. Panama hat, cravat.
Saturday, town square, approaches
teenaged dad with infant in pushchair.

Old gives New the big hello,
and waving with a whole-arm motion,
suggests: a lifetime's arc, the globe,

the sun's diurnal course –
goodbye is in there, too – grandiloquent
as ceremonies of first and last should be.

Not with bluest baby-gro,
or gilt-edged card, or gaudiest baptism,
was ever better welcome given.

# Cattle Among Trees

Stolid curiosity inclines its head,
and ruffles its matted hide.
Life is grass. No lesser argument
intrudes. Cuyp's cows or Virgil's
would have stared as loftily,
tails casually fly-whisking
of their own accord.
Zen masters might grace the shade
with the same unpetty silence.
There's time for everything:
in the dusk, need
saunters slowly after need,
for movement, watering, shelter.
Jaws revolve, teats sag like bagpipes.
Panic will be as rare
as the stinging of hail.
'Alone' is a freak of the farmer's.
It's deceptive. It looks like eternity.
One, various Cow.

## Mrs Hues

Mounted on a fine bay gelding, dressed as a gentleman…
*your money instantly, or you are a dead man…*
Captured, Mrs Hues 'owned she was a woman',
thus admitting, my lord, that she had no business
with pistols, or a stranger's 200 guineas.
No business, certainly, with hanging. I present to you
Mrs Hues, not a girl on the razzle, a craver of thrills,
a vendeuse of nocturnal wares, but a bold heart, and a lover
of Mr Hues, who would sit by a guttering hearth
over a hot posset, and a copy of *The Vicar of Wakefield*,
awaiting the distant *tuppety tuppety* of hooves.

# Aura

A winter sun is fingering the stalls,
slowly lightening, like milk in tea,
the plaster busts of Elvis,
Kowloon tartan scarves.

A vendor on the tarmac grips
a bag, shower-curtain thick.
His face, out of an abbatoir,
is garish with the cold, and now

there's company: a woman
rigid as a crane, an elder Fury
in descent, who angles fiercely for
a bargain lime-green double-pack,

as he rips, and splits the bag
into murky veils. Shadows fuse:
blunt animal, and flayed machine.
All this occurs in the no-time of a glance.

Behind them a granite sky is streaked
with fissures like a ruined plinth.
Their flurried moment lasts,
frozen with that long violence.

# Tinnitus

It's hardly like losing an eye, you couldn't sue,
but one pundit reckons that silence is God; if so,
I'm godless, and nostalgic for the nights I listened
from the lair of the streets, to the starry window.

Instead what I learn and learn is a restlessness,
as supplanting the peace, a demonic sentinel leans
in the open arch of perception, whirring his barbed tail.
I get things done, like Sisyphus. Not even that.

Like some wan woman, washing her hair in the Styx.

# Things

The dumb things, the laggard shoes and keys,
in the aftermath as the hall light
strafes the bedroom floor
through an opening door.

Out of a glutted backpack, these sure things,
witness to the body and its derelictions:
T-shirts snug as bedtime prayer,
socks plotting out their even destinations.

The useful things, so unintelligent
compared to the body's metropolitans –
the jazzy hormones and glib blood cells –
but faithful, so faithful.

To hand, foreswearing telephoned goodbyes,
meeting the skin unreservedly.
These things. It's not through them
that negation moves, this chill.

# Twilight

Nettled, half-ablaze,
she stumped along shop windows.

It was either tat, or rosy come-ons,
and in the glass, the beetling selves
hissed, and multiplied.

At one end of the high road,
a sky like moleskin paled
to the colour of water.

She slowed, and stood
for nothing – mottled ambergris,
the smog's violet wash – a deepening

that went on, assuring with the mildest touch,
*twilight, this is how it could be done.*

## Happy Hour

Three girls meander down Newington.
One commands thickly, *let the lady pass.*
They turn to consider me with incurious eyes.

They move off awry, like a pantomime horse.
The traffic croons home. Three rouged-up dolls
meditate hard and numbly at shop windows.

Whatever thrashes round in them, sleeps.
They totter on spikes, in frocks, amiably swearing,
down that leafy, singing lane.

# Cement Mixer

All afternoon,
I've been captive to its
*nnnn – naa – nnnn*,
the sound of toil.

Workaholic, dogged,
if it pauses for a minute,
its vitals whiten into rock:
it only rotates to sustain

the old sloppiness
of possibility; the jellyfish gleam.
Whether the form intended
is an overpass in Swindon

or the Glasgow School of Art,
a bollard or a sundial,
matters not. A dog's paw
might be as eligible

for attention. When it pours
it goes native, adapting itself.
That's the cunning.
That's the fly-trap,

care, and evasions
notwithstanding: permanency,
or what could pass for
permanency with us.

## Telegraph Pole

A telegraph pole rides prone
on a flatbed truck,
its periwig awry, the white
ceramic conductors twined with rust –
creosoted, splintered tree of knowledge,
draped with jackdaw litter, hung with talk.

It fell last night, in the gale,
and rides through burnished streets
to the lumber yard.

Black wires underscore the horizon.
Poles march over the reedbed,
rootless, and branchless.
Clamped horizontal to the lorry bed,
Ajax borne off on the field of Troy.

## Plato Said

Strumming Parthian slave girls,
spikenard-drenched actors:
it's the glamour dismays me:
whining 'Achilles'
is a poor example to youth.
'Helen' won't keep Sparta
from nipping at the borders.

A lie is a lie is a lie,
*except for the welfare of the state.*
*Your cave itself is metaphorical.*
*You covet glamour*
*for mere wisps of thought.*
*A rose is not capitalised.*

It's the randomness that appals.
A farmer's stud chases
a young rhapsodist: soon,
every epode bears the image of a bull.
He sings *aroma* instead of *agatha*
(today he prefers the labial),
yet pretends to honeyed immortality...

*And so we live –*
Such are your versifiers.
*And so we live,*
*in the shimmer on Aegea's water.*

## Lucifer, Baby

*Lucifer, baby, you're in the dark age.*
*You're the woolly mammoth, music hall.*
*Evil these days, it's event, not presence,*
*no one guy gets to star, however screwball.*

So Lucifer hangs about the studios
wearing black like iridescent scales,
and when he sees the dish, or doxy
of his dreams, sheds twenty years,
and fleet of foot, moves in,
as arch-controller, Lucifer-by-proxy.

His are the shadows dappling the canal,
the grip returning thunderbolts;
everything that's flung at him: his the slur
of treacle over answerphones;
night sweats, flies, and whisperings,
the skull in a builder's skip.

Lucifer consumes his lovers quite –
burnt match – and lays them down
between spavined brolly and bent ferrule,
spatchcocked, to hiss of mortal failures.
They go out pearly, lightened of themselves.
He drums them back to school.

*Night drawing in, I stop for breath.*
*Look at the pink above the roofs!*
*Your lies are prettier than anybody's truths,*
*Lucifer – and what was that you said, again?*

# The Passage

In the passage between houses,
a rucksack gaped in the dirt, revealing
a milkpan, a toy kettle,
and a greenish, flat bottle of olive oil.

When I came up that narrow way again,
the rucksack was gone.
The cooking things lay absurd, under a wisteria.
I took the olive oil home.

The next time I climbed there,
the kettle had been kicked down
all 25 steps, and the milk pan
resembled a bopeep sunhat.

But today the passage undulates free
between the old-rose bricks,
the dark August leaves parting
for turrets, and captains' walks,

and a sliver of turquoise,
on which an immaculate sail
rides motionless, a small white yacht
whose invisible hull

winks, diamond, down the coast,
and what could it be signalling?
Never distress, the sea is too serene.
It must be the sun, its last late beam,

exiled, hailing, *goodbye*.

# Fire Tongs

I was down the oubliette once.
Couldn't see forward or back,
and slumped there, helpless.
Wait, misery said, wait,

and I saw, without light, a pair
of cast iron fire tongs,
and squatted, as blank as a beast,
in front of *fire tongs, fire tongs*,

until the mind ran up panting
through an unsensed door,
and I heard myself complain
of being caught between friend

and friend (intent on their
own causes, blind towards me),
as the dumb wood started
and sang out, a blue flame.

## A Right Pair

The gloves, due to be lost, have gone to their assignation,
sprawling on a Tube platform, or in a telephone kiosk,
aghast at the naked hands of the hired ladies;
murmuring of how they felt dirty, like serfs, I was in
and out at my own discretion. They'd lie
caressing my lap, or dangling from my grip like orphans.
Well, they knew I had a heart: they'd felt its obligato
tremoring at a wrist, but never quite benefited (or so
the woolly muttering went) but just see how they fare,
one ingesting the faint filth of shoes, tossed prone on the pavement;
its mate on a railing spike, skewed, saluting all comers.

# Nocturne

Great aunts in wicker armchairs,
snow drifts, a pink 50s kitchen.
Throaty, Victorian triumph. *Gin!*
They were here all the time,

The old affections, they rise like bruises.
I lie face up on the bed.
Even the yellow dog we had
finds her way back, muddied, done in.

The tree in the alley dangles its claws
over the green, and ghostly blooms.
The sky, night-streaked and opaque,
turns outward to the ignorant distances.

# Mole

A farmer beckoned on the roadside.
Wales, Christmas. I was an au pair.
I wound down the passenger's window
as a large, dead mole fell into my lap —
a fitting gift for the young aspirant,
although I didn't appreciate it then.

A role model, you might even say:
a night-eyed, tenacious tunnel-digger
at work in the sodden cold;
piling through regardless
of the rocks, and owls, and foxes,
and the farmer, laughing, by.

# Glass

You clambered into that glass of whisky
as the station bar was about to shut –
the tables curiously leaning into each other
like mates in a photo; the shutters scraped down,
the broom and dustpan flourished
with French hilarity, like the barman's goodbyes –
after a string of comforts, whiskys, Guinness,
heading off to pied-à-terre lodgings in Richmond:
no need for the unremarkable courage of the Dutch,
no glints in it, you are loved.

## The Fire Hills

I've laboured up the stone path
to the Fire Hills,
through black stream beds and gorse track,
overtaking a man with a nubbled stick,
and overtaken by sinewy fell runners.

The cliffs, the winking sea,
are old beyond enduring;
the flux makes me its momentary darling,
but I'm as they are, as old as they are,
hurrying towards other, and other.

# Move

It's not easy to walk the streets in this state.
A bleached blond guy holding hands with his boy love,
tells me to MOVE.

I remonstrate. I am moving, shadowed and thwarted
by the singular gravity of others.
(Cue for the screwing up of his face in exaggerated contempt.)

Well you may ask what brought this on.
Tonight it sings off me.
I'm bared to the pith, to the green quick.

Drunks, touts, and scamsters
approach, to introduce themselves
on wet curbstones.

# Writer's Breviary

## 1 *With Strangers*

Disuse thickens the voice. This *here*
is a long step away from the natural,
from the creased snapshot of home,
and the reliable mate. It's a gamble.

It's vainglory, this plying for evanescence,
syntax like a murmurous twist in the gut –
not an actual sentence, nor for life,
but possibly a clause too far.

## 2 *Three Kinds of Making*

Sticks on a mossy bank connive
at the meanest of fences.
A crooked line ends with an apple blossom.
The maker has left no further trace of himself.

The farmer's hailing words in the leaf-gloom:
lit windows, extinct at midnight;
the whiteness of a page, as painted light.

## 3 *The Writer and Heraclitus*

Stand on its mossy ledges twice?
To stand here once is an endeavour.
Any certainty's been bartered for a song –
for less, tight runes, an insect discipline –
although overhead, a host of birds,
*extempore*, fearlessly call.

## Shadow Book

She made a shadow book, and put in it
taboo things: hungers, ancient fears
steeped in other fears, already black.
No pictures; words invariably opaque.
Edited by – to say, time, would be too pat.
Certainly the title page was blank.
As for readers, one would be too many.
She closed it tight. It floated crookedly
down the long stream, the opposite of Moses
in his basket, taking every *The End* with it.
It won't dissolve, or petrify, or open.
There are things like that. There need to be –
closed books, and dreamless sleep.

## Chase

Lately the athletic gangsters and the beasts
of nightmare have fallen back
and let me run, aborigine,
pelting after the small game;

chasing a cygnet, last night,
the hard length of the road;
negotiating stacked boxes and bruised fruit,
for a bit of grey fluff that

evaded, tumbled soft, and when
I finally, peacably, closed my hand
I owned...a swatch of dust, as a cat slunk by,
knowing more than it pretended.

# Outcome

Dawn shelter in the station waiting-room,
the spoils of night as dregs of tea,
the restless hand as porter's broom,
the Nile of touch as postcard of the sea.

The hurried voice as beating rain,
the driven breath as stubbed-out-on-the-floor,
the savaged clothes as orderly again.
The nerves' entente as thunder by the door.

## *from* **The Good Weekend**

Time to ogle the plaster rose, find a pub:
brass taps, and thumpety-thump in the jukebox.
Miss Muzak had swallowed a jackhammer.
What's that shite I yell above the heads
when an apparition rose like genie
exited from lamp, and towered there incarnate:
no helpful spirit, alas, full twenty stone,
and said, who are you calling shite?

Not you, I said. Not you.

London in twilight:
the pigeon-grey river,
Cleopatra's blackened needle,
a palette of greys,
low strands of light,
the first night of my weekend

and stand in the cheerful midnight street,
a rock in the stream off the night buses,

then kip down under billowing pink
rhododendrons
for a couple of cold hours.

And up, rigid,
to the smell of the black earth,
and skirting the fence to avoid the keepers,
and walking to warm myself.

Jesus will it be dawn.


Poring for coins in a backstreet gutter
a ginger cat nuzzling,
under the shut-eyed houses,

turn again –

turn again,

and sit athwart the pedestrian bridge, feet splayed, and watch
the slim blue spires of earliest morning;
eating the unadorned bread, and greet the northern wanderer
as it hurtles unstinting now and lit
with dawn that sleekly rides its black full-throttled heart of fury –

timely,
the 5:03.

# The Steps

She diminished the man.

She voodoo'd him.
Fear made her dream him
tiny, ant-like.

She dreamed she lost him
on the stair.
It would have taken him a year
to find his way up.

Each step would have loomed
like Annapurna.

Elated, at the top,
he'd have to face
the soft rucks and furls
of her clothes, strewn,
islanded in the hall.

He'd need to sling
his rope, one hair,
through the white plains of dust,
bridge a ravine
to the next floorboard,

and slay his fear
of that original woman,
face abutting the clouds.

Most of all, could he forgive
a final craning vision
of her, as monster,
monolith – before entering,

restored, as a man?

# Fort DeWitt

*Crack!* It's the hour of parade
in Fort DeWitt's unblemished neighbourhood
of barbecues, and Safeway's opulent chill.

White-gloved soldiers file
in and out, and muscular recruits
pretend to die, at calisthenics.

Not a blade of grass awry,
not a scuff-mark. Behind the shutters
of the military post office, a rasping voice:

'If he thinks he can fire me
because some crazy woman in Panama
says I stole mail from a sack,

then he can shove it, he'll find out.'
And now the helicopter's stuttering descent;
the staid approach of horses.

# The Awkward Guest

### I

The awkward guest cried *murder!*
into the round agog of the courtyard well.
A single self, a dark and distant girl,
rippled deep, as if to disappear...


### II

The old house drew its luck from a mason's hen:
a pagan Tudor offering, sealed in a beam,
dry bones with beak agape.

In a trickle of days, the new wing went up,
navvies on Dexedrine, foreman grey,
Sir Jack's in London, back presently.

Meanwhile his wife picks quietly
between the stacks of dusty pine,
hiding her face in her hand.

She's eaten of a herb called *all-her-fault*,
and another called *heart's-fear*.
They can never build it big enough.


### III

The guest could have sailed off
for the small ports that day,
of Penicuik, Dalkeith, Auchendinny –
returning, damp and bicycle-clipped,

with *Rob Roy*, or a Campbell tartan,
from the Heart Fund charity shop;
or a crystal shot glass, or a pine cone;
or a ginger man for tea.

But hers was the less explicable mission,
cold chronicler in a guest room,
a rag-tag of litter chasing itself down a rat-run
from Archway Tower, to station –

while outside a meadow gleamed with rain,
the white May Candlemas amassing
in glens, dells, blood-red sandstone crevices.
She worked on at her desk, alone.

The ghost of the Gothic peered in:
'Zounds! Leave off that detective trash!
Who needs another? I am venerable
and lonely. The bats attend me!'

A relic of the Real snorted,
'Oh, please, *your* acolytes are many,
if bloodless, and unsociable.
More difficult by far, to say what is.'

…but at that moment there were,
at once, actual footsteps
and a knock of doom,
and her hostess-fair, walked in.


### IV

The lived *I* being above all, diffuse,
poised in the door of all its open rooms,
a rebus; an Egyptian eye, vase water –
to say *I vow*, is like kneading mist,
but there is another, tangible verb.

That afternoon, she watched it prove
agile, intent, as water bead, fleet
down the rim,
journeying to acknowledge the other.

# The Elements

A small flame flings itself about,
a wittering, an astronaut,
riding the kindled air above
the burgundy chrysanthemum.

The flame, the red, the window view,
are the locus, fine netting for a haul
of happiness in a peopled room –
but mind is more than merely eye.

Mind is also fingers, primed
at once to manoeuvre, and move.
Include, then, that beat-up bicycle outside,
in the failing evening.

## China Head

*a version of pastoral*

On the edge of a great estate,
I found a little china head,
staring up through the blue speedwell;
a straw-hatted boy, Italianate,
freckled with dirt.

The keeper's donkeys nudge the fence
another spring, and April's mud
breeds vetch, and campion.
The shepherd gazes out, at bloody births
and undistinguished deaths.

Secure now in the boggy earth,
with rootlings for a coverlet,
against tremors of the figurine,
as piquet players fled for breath
out to the flowery borders of a myth –

indignities of nature irk him less
than these, the fractious chatelaines
and weary planters – wan
as any Dresden shepherdess –
intoning hyacynthine verse,

while toilers raised the great gazebo,
the ha-ha, maze and parapet;
nameless, dug the lily ponds,
until language danced cotillion, slow,
if brightly, from the burnt château.

If, beguiled by a general thaw, he ever
yearns to resurrect, he'll need his lines
reworked for him, democratised in fact; a bower
of vines against the April blast:
the deluge, now, blessing the wanderer.

FROM

# Timing

(1997)

# On the Holloway Road

Where then now, Jack Kerouac?
Down some reeling American valley
to Denver city;

San Fran Hoboken Mexico; old Jonah
in the sweltering gut,
bleached with a million fishes – ?

Come to the Holloway Road
Jack; you & any angels *en passant*,
the Roman Great North Way,

rich in wizened rubbish sacks,
furtive Greek card games; two or three
fast fooders, with TV zap and shine;

burrow in the velvet pubs of Celtic fiddle swing,
join the Secular Society and the Merchant Seamen;
circle the centrepoint of language

for zanzibars of meaning in this grey,
hero of sensations. Descend
to our foggy east, reddened with Dharma light.

# The Narrows

*May I ask you a question?*
A taxi driver to the mirror overhead.
*What is there beside work and sleep?*
The cab lolloped over a speed bump.

*Pleasures go by and then we're old.*
We slowed to a dieseled stasis.
Cab and man were shades of black,
handing me a Xeroxed sheet,

THE PURSUIT OF HAPPINESS.
I read it, leaning in at the meter light.
I can't remember what it said.
He was running the narrows quite alone.

I didn't have the nerve to tip.
With that muttering ease of cabs,
he drove off to confound another soul,
turning right on the station road.

# The Anaesthetist

This rubber pump in my hand sighs, pants, and wheezes
for you, my dear. Nighty-night, Ms Prynn.
Forbuoy approaches to wheel you in.
He is the theatre orderly. He *is* theatrical,

whipping off the dark green sheet like a tablecloth,
leaving you with nothing much to fall back on.
You are well under now, a gleaming cold matron.
Forbuoy is messing about with his pink slop.

The surgeon pulls latex over his finger joints;
the nurse displays her swift knives and forks.
Forbuoy and his shadow start to snigger, the oiks,
in the holy second of waiting.

The present, powerful, naked Ms Prynn
glows and is bold, illumined further
by the big lamp lowered like a flying saucer
as it hovers, stops.

Then round that star-lit table we are all drawn in.
You are turned and covered; your back basted pink.
I touch your wrist, while you stumble in your Hades walk,
Ms Prynn, at the first, sharp rocks.

# Testament

To my last technician,
I leave this flaming skeleton.

I like you better
than a doctor, or a hairdresser.

My leaving do's a blast, a whirl,
I'm a party girl,

Nude and ablaze like a tree,
one spectacular x-ray.

Look up from the gauges, be a voyeur,
a happy pyro-connoisseur,

But don't think to make free
with the calcine ash, the grit of me –

That's for a feeling hand,
or the wind.

# The Hen Night Club's Last Supper

Take this bread roll and this
Sangria cup in remembrance that we
are one another's blood,
and come from women's body.

Drink, and eat tonight, my chucks,
in solidarity,
for dawn affrays with bloody men
in their obstinate beauty.

Go bravely into the world of snooker halls,
Downing Street and the packet of three.
*Nil carborundum*, bless the Marks,
and bless this company.

## Talkers

I've met two kinds of talkers.
The one has undoubtedly suffered –
call it a birth trauma that lasts
seventy, eighty years.
Even the matter of which bus to catch
hurts them, they must talk it out.

The other isn't certain if they themselves
are real, but the mind, at least,
is a fountain, reaching and flourishing
when anyone nudges the pump-switch –
a caretaker, say, who at once discovers
in what profusion lonely love abounds.

# Returning to the Park in July

In April the goslings scattered
across the pavement – pell-mell
golden gusts of alive – where? gone
to low-slung, stately geese
poking about in muck like weekend royals,
or disembarking from the lowest dockside
*kerplop*, and gliding, beaks to the air,
assured, and never again astonished, never
fleeing to the shade and back between
the iron railings and the pond.

# Queynt

Hostage to the phalli,
where are your celebrations?
In the delivery suite;
among the porn queens?

Blood-warm and sea-brine,
maroon luxurious
rupture, your monuments
aren't theirs,

columns and Concorde; you've
only you, strong
as grass, sly mouth. Lewd
old thing.

# Leaf

Whorled and buckled
in the bawling sun, it turns
as brash as carnival,

staining itself cerise,
baroque and charred,
uncurling from the vine,

it eddies through nets of green
to a summer ground, heaped
with flames that have aged and ended.

# Star

I raise my forearm against the lens and they never get me.
Paparazzi stunts, hack sermons don't matter – or didn't
until the *döppelganger*, an LA shark dead-ringing for me,
started bluffing his way into Le Caprice or Jerry's.

This guy had a past, teen-aged girls, other rumours,
to wreck a White House soiree, drop the sponsors in Swanee.
I took some advice, the palmist, the clinic, a Monterey lawyer.
I tracked this jerk down a restaurant alley: wrong I.D.

The guy who turned around with a frown was a third man,
a fan, who wore my twenty-year old face on his t-shirt.
Then I saw the glint of the piece. Do you know who I am,
I asked, but his eye was exact. Point-blank, in fact.

My twin copped it too and it's him they remember.
I'm in limbo, safe, where no one knows me. Many mansions –
forget it, this is more like a cell, lightless
and senseless, but private: oblivion. The way I like it.

# Cigarettes

Brand X, the brand
of habitual beauty
– the wrist-flicked match,

the airy signature,
plush o's of smoke –
marks the man

that closest family visit,
with grapes,
and twenty Bensons in a purse;

who'd been greedy for nothing
exotic, like the real
Golden Virginia –

just local pleasures,
round the block.
Those little trips.

# £5 Haircut

No cup of tea, no blow-driers, no *conversazione*,
no lacquered bobs shining from magazines.

Buzz-cut young men step up one after another.
My head is pushed into the penitent position.

A hairshirt begins its wheedling under my collar,
as the silver shears divest me

of the human, which, flittering to the base
of the clinical chair, heaps softly.

# Timing

Light hosanna'd in the mirrors.
We were double, multiple; but our quadrille
ended when you bowed and faded.

This evening in you walked – foot-sore, apologetic.
A minstrel, out of tune.
The sun had gone in, the room was brown

through the rattan blinds,
and I'm no coy languisher, no Penelope.
I'd done my scribbling in the book of you.

# Egg

This is the thing to hunt in the Easter grass.
On the eye it's merciless,
red and hard like a tuber – or nothing at all,
a cicada's carapace.

It has taken a life to prepare,
like the golden Fabergé the poor goose died to inherit.

I want it shattered:
a yellow smear and a spot of blood
from which the lean cockerel grows, can still grow,
feathering its cry.

## Spunk Talking

When men are belligerent or crude,
it's spunk talking, it's come come up for a verbal interlude:
*in your face Jack, get shagged, get screwed, get your tits out,*
*get him, lads, bugger that, hands off, just you try it,*
*you're nicked, left hook, nice one Eric, hammer hard,*
*shaft him, stitch that, do you want to get laid or not, red card.*
Spunk speaks in gutterals, with verbs. No parentheses.
Spunk's a young con crazy to break from Alcatraz.
Sonny, you'll go feet first. So spunk has to sing,
hoarsely, the *Song of the Volga Boatmen, I am an Anarchist,*
the Troggs' *Wild Thing.*
Cynthia Payne said, after her researches, not to be debunked,
that men are appreciably nicer when de-spunked.
Before time began the void revolved, as smooth and bored
as an egg, when a tiny ragged crack appeared,
and the world exploded like an umpire's shout,
as the primal spunk of the cosmos bellowed OUT.

# Play On

Football and poems
are grace and havoc.
Pure attar of futility.
Nothing can come of it.
Nothing. I love that.

The kit is blood-red,
the substitutions ruthless,
the heroes French, or Celt.
A hydra-head roars
at their blazing backs:

the lines exultant, loping,
as they pass, and re-pass –
but there is one man, one
vexed and critical eye,
their nemesis.

Nevertheless,
they run, as if
their sensual, streaming
argument could persuade
that worrier to leap aside

from the nets of sense,
and watch them send
his beaten envoy home
on a green field;
in the grace of one poem.

# Thaw

You tease us, charmer.
AWOL for weeks together,
when the brusque Siberian complains.

But settling to warmth, we
marvel at your leniency,
your entrance braceleted in light.

Then everyone alive's your advocate.

# Two Birds

There were two dead birds,
featherless young,
on the garden bricks this morning.

They were cold and blue –
but even so distrait, those
rude embryos

refused, with open beaks,
to enter the black plastic sack.
The earth will make

something of them.
She's the fecund one.
Why can't I be her handmaiden,

instead of writing out
these frail receipts – why not locate
my little plot, and live on it?

## Bella Dora

Bella Dora, a patient at the Institute of Calm,
used to look too long at the sun.
She wanted to go blind, she said, troubling the nurses,
so that someone will take care of me.
Round-eyed, she stood among the parked cars and seemed,
with her head tipped back, to be drinking sunlight.
When her wealthy family flared onto the ward
she followed them demurely,
but she wanted to age into their imperious marshal
with a white baton, their shadow walking before them;
to demand love, to accept it without shame.

# Highbury Fields

It was VE day.
The beacon shrieked at the god of war,
this is what we do for excitement here, okay?

The coconut shy, the Chinese noodle treats,
the Crooked House for Kids, the mayor's
rites of torch;

pensioners in razzle hats, the conga line
of red-gold faces, and this flame
nattering at the sky for us –

Then a man with a grievance hurtled towards the fire.
Children and grown-ups craned in a ring
to watch running, cursing firemen

snatch him from the flames; bundle him off unsinged
to broadcast calming voices –
but we'd seen, and drunk. War had won.

# Blitz

'In '41 it got so bad
every city morgue was full.
We couldn't unload our lot,
burned most of 'em, poor
buggers, and fragmentary.
We had to stack 'em in the dugout,
on the high bunks.
I sat on a cot while Archie
boiled us up three mugs, brown
as boots. Then a near hit
rocked the joists.
That one rattled us,
Bev the driver, Archie and me –
you could hear the bones jar
against the wood,
and the spoon jingling
in the sugar billy...'

# Air Ambulance

They came running to the creature
cogitating on the hill. A man had fallen
from a window, but they weren't here for blood.
A policeman easily cleared the stretcher's way.

Strapped-down and red-blanketed, he'd
brought them their luck: this whirling visitant
that steadied itself, conferred,
and lifted above the glorious noisy wind;

that tilted, took on the rights of air and shot
itself as from a crossbow, cleanly south. Far off
it looked the thing it was. They drifted back,
for tea and TV, nearly emptying the park.

# The Outlands

I've been walking the outlands of the self,
recording its cold impasses and its wounds,
its mudflats and fervent suns and thrashing water.
Someone had hung out bangles on the stunted
trees over the wallows. I nearly sank bejewelled –
then headed north-west to where the howls subside
at zero, and the moon loses its smudged nimbus.
Where I hear of remarkable cities.

# Sunset Grill

(1993)

# Pools

He told a tolerant mike that things wouldn't change much.
Caught in the cameras' freeze, through the chat
And clink of the milling PR boys,
The wife stood working his hand like billyo.

Are you a winner? a magazine asked. He'd said no.
Behind the TV a generous sun touched a hill
As they'd hushed, listening for the child's cry.
Consoles and bedroom suites lined up to cheer.

They broke through the door, led by the wide-toothed compère.
The sky was uncannily white, the sky that a newt puzzles under,
Circling its grass-lined bowl.
With her arm in his, he mumbled it would be all right.

# Baby Tony at Al's Café

The gangling child, outgrowing babyhood
Lolls on his pushchair, a seaside toff.
Fate's pinned him here as audience
To the waiter's act with knives,
And left a consoling bottle out of reach.
His pre-prandial remarks conclude
In a surging *Dies Irae*: the waiter,
A family man, retrieves it where it lies.
Babe slugs it back, fish-eyed through the smoke.
His mother pauses from volubility to dote,
Swooping aside before the sentence drops.
Our man has tasted everything once.
He gets another chip, tests it with his mouth,
Rolling it slowly round like a panatella.

# England Nil

The advance to Hamburg broke with all the plans.
Doug spelled them out in Luton Friday night.
Someone had ballsed it up. A dozen vans
Waited in convoy, ringside. Blue and white
We stumbled through. The beer
When we found it in that piss-hole of jerries
Was all we needed. Who won the war,
Anyway? Who nuked Dresden? Two fairies
Skittered behind the bar, talking Kraut
Or maybe Arabic. We clocked the poison
Smiles and chanted till the SS threw us out.
Stuttgart was a tea-party to this. One
By one they've nicked us, berserk with fear.
You've been Englished but you won't forget it, never.

# Burst

The sort of place that waits to become someone's past,
Is Lugworth Council's Mental Health Drop-in Centre.
She moves through the invisible hunched backs and stigmata
With the sanctity of the fit.
He attends irregularly, in a suit;
Carries her globular cameo back to his flat.

He's not that daft: she's a Tokyo Rose, hybrid, trained for this.
You could follow her voice for months without connection.
One bland day he sees her shopping with the mythical husband.
Both hello generously, not realising the transgression,
And the damned thing bursts over his part of the building,
A godawful mess but too thin even to drown in.

# Her Retirement

Just a little party, nothing swank,
I told the founder, but you know Mr B.
There are so many of you here to thank.

I leave you the later tube trains, dank
At the hand-rails from a human sea,
Dreaming down to Morden via Bank.

I've homed quietly to port while others sank,
By keeping at my stenography.
There are so many of you here to thank.

I scan the backs of houses, rank on rank:
The comfy lamps, the oblique misery
Streaming down to Morden via Bank.

Our gardens keep us from the abyss, I think.
With the cheque I'll buy a trellis, or a tree.
There are so many of you here to thank.

And unaccustomed as I am to drink,
I toast you all who follow me
– There are so many of you here to thank –
In dreaming down to Morden, via Bank.

# Sacrificial Wolf

The careful suburban dead turn their backs
On this squat of sodden grass,
Hedged by the Finchley traffic:
The vicar poised like a prowhead
Over the shameless pit, answered
By a hectoring gull. It brings back
The afternoons in the dry houses,
The hostels and clinic waiting-rooms,
When you with the cor anglais of a shout
Parted the smokers' fug,
Flattering social workers with quotes
From Wilde or Krishnamurti –
Such was the splendour and disgrace
That only a few of us have come to light
Our makeshift Roman candles, bitten shy:
An elegy, my friend, dear wolf,
Being just your sort of con.

# Virginian Arcady

My muse came up from the creek,
Taller than a man in the speckled shade,
Where crayfish imitate tiny stones,
And the brisk water plays.

Reckon it was a muse, being so
Ringletty and fair, with a child's eye.
In her head-dress bitter, living grapes
Nest on the wild vine.

Strolling the bogged paths
Of the bottom field, apart by armslength,
She talked low, reproachful, pretty:
Said I don't love her enough.

## Christmas Break

We've floored it from London.
The bridge winches up; the moat bares
To green algae silk, kitchen relics,
The bones of suicides.

The snow, fine as bride's
Fine lace, stacks up its trousseau:
A terrain in bedsheets, smoothed from memory.
The town's dead as midnight.

Rushing the houses of the estate,
The wind skims the roof
Like a bruising hand.
From now, a dining-table

Accommodates six at Scrabble
And a week's career beneath
The fairy lights: a family circuit
Closing like a wreath.

# The Uni-Gym

At a shout to a disco drum, the women dance
In sorbet cotton knits. Sweat darkening
On spines, they bend and reach.

In the stone chill of the gym downstairs,
Weightlifters howl, as if for sex,
Or pace, furtive in the room-sized mirror,

To meet gingerly in bed. His density
Helps him feel safer from the likes of her –
Whose heart is stronger now, and unforgiving.

# Flynn

I saw Flynn from the 14 bus
Launched from Mecca's,
Trudging towards Kings Cross.

He's been livelier, last week
Gesturing hugely in the bra boutique
(I kissed him, had to take it back.)

I mouthe while his body talks, shameless.
Tight shoulders, sentry's head –
We've gone further than he intended.

Even crying in my arms, any sense of us
Eludes him like luxury. I rap the glass
With my ring. He doesn't see me.

# Springfield, Virginia

Colonels live there, commuters to the Pentagon
In sweetly-named estates: King's Park, Orange Wood.
Springfield proper is a set of asphalt lots,
A catch-all town for realtors and mail.

At Peoples Drug, and the fast-food joints,
The hands popping open the cylinders of change
Hail from Vietnam or Nicaragua, arrivistes
Wondering at the sourness of God's people.

The high schoool kids who used to do the jobs
Were white, immune to history:
Andy Sulick, sheepish in a Big Ranch Stetson hat,
A row of enforced dim smiles at Burger Chef.

Eight hundred graduated in '71. That night,
Crawling the backroads, jumping in and out
Of unfamiliar cars, I found a party at a shack.
A boy mashed me against the lean-to floor.

Along the wooded road lightning bugs flared
Like drunks with matches, seeing their way home,
And whipperwills nagged the sleeper
Until a dawn as pink and blue as litmus paper.

# Seventeen Year Locust or Magicicada

As a nymph it latches for a stark
Seventeen years on a knuckled root,
Blind and hugely feeding
Hostage to the dark.

A swelling ache
Corkscrews it from the ground,
To hug the nearest vertical,
Squaddie out of bivouac,

And burst the carcass, dangled
Like a pilot from a one-seater
With flaccid wings, bug eyes,
And goggled head.

Hardening, it starts to pull
Free; by dawn it flies,
Fuelled just long enough for sex:
A single churring in the red maple.

## M3

Mean as a length of flex, it snubs the B road,
Disliking breakdown and hiker, impedimenta;
Droning the highway code
At shuddering lorries, and the reps for shampoo,
Blurring southward to the postcard rack
And coffee on the lido.

As time stripped down to mere emergency,
It tarmacs older memories of sense,
Of littering picnic; of plum tree,
Rooks, and manure,
Nerves like a harp in the blown high grass.
Inland, it simply hands over.

# Faith Healers

This could be the mind's antechamber:
Skylight, pre-war folding chairs, a stand of books,
The *Psychic News*, a hand-penned plea, DONATIONS:
Against each wall a lame hope waiting.

The ends of her sparse hair are a failed red,
She's stout and leads a shambling Alsatian.
'Through the veil' a limpid Jesus lifts his eyes
Above the nursery warmth, the funk of flowers.

The heaters of the clerestory
Burn among the eaves, vivid as lollies.
Patients play stone crusaders on the spindly beds.
The healers in their grocery macs

Press forehead, gut and thighs
Like John who spent his grace on strays
In a sirocco, a name for talisman.
They tend the dog, lay hands on anyone.

## Nude Descending a Stair

It's 2 A.M. when the placid telephone shrieks.
A silhouette floats over the fly-posted shops,

and enters: a game of toy soldiers,
you'd think to hear them talk, descending

to a basement hung with nylon fetters,
with an unknown atmosphere, and speech.

To hear them talk – but these rarely do,
above water. We goggle in a movie-house;

co-opt their stylish silence, frame by frame.
*For beauty*, rubbish – they are just afraid.

## Athletic

I've stripped down to the clean athletic.
Even blood relatives fall away. Their trace
Is a spidery map of obligations,
And a compass needle, flitting towards normalcy.
I have my deadlines; my coldwater diet.
The early freshness has burned off,
Although the heart works double time.
Power is its priority, not love.
It is red and rude to the egg's melancholy,
Sacrificing her gladly. My face fits me,
These days, like a glove of pig leather,
And hides the arrogant boy
With the fear of long meetings.
The one thing he knows how to do is destroy.

## Sister Dread

The future unself, that starts with me,
The sexless yellowing sister,
Bored with her safe plot under the roses,
Sets me problems of the cryptic type.
She fancies herself a teacher.

How gratifying to see me sweat.
She's a bundle of sticks, no monster.
Having to go through the stage of effluvium
She hates the smell:
I stick in the craw of her tidy eternity.

She thinks she is omnivorous, although
I have my unassailable territory.
Reduced to pulling hideous faces through glass,
She'd prefer to believe that I never was
Her sitting tenant, but fact is fact.

## Homage to Jean Rhys

At the corner table, perusing a face
In unimproving colours,
Brandy, absinthe, Cinzano,

Latticed by the rudeness
Of strangers, shut portcullis,
Madam whispers

To a passing gentleman
Who has, he's afraid, to dash:
Words are bandages.

The reader peers, permitted like
A medical student.
She's forgotten him.

Swaddled tight, she'll black out
Harmlessly, unhelped:
A walking Montmartre ghost,

Ex-chorus girl, anglaise,
Vieille, ex-ex.
No one can get in or out.

# Streambed

What was once bird
Is a fan of grey feathers,
Wavering on the streambed,
A few feet from the Thames.

It ate a barleycorn, and now
The green blade is eating it,
Vivid and cruel
As some young can be.

The blue-lit chub
Course through the shallows.
The down flutters,
Pinioned by the shoots.

An old party on the footbridge
Lingering after others,
Following the fish,
Ignores the former bird.

# A Day Out in Berkshire

The trundling air balloon turns and preens
Against blue clemency. The buds were metal
When we crouched here among the fag-ends,

A late day when you turned aside
At the station platform, with boy's eyes:
It was warmer then than now, warm

As when a woman wooed a snake
That whispered to her – *time* – and slid,
A tremor in the fields, a single track.

Then Adam had to die, to save the crops;
Eve ruled, a goddess but not immortal,
And love sleeps in its attenuated state

Of splendour after the rosé, two good bottles;
You anchored in my blood, dumb dream-boat,
Not telling why I have to dream instead.

# The Madam

We wanted to be tough, to rope the bleating rams
Into a dread spectacular!
The last raid on the house felt like a game.
I preferred prison meals and circuit walks
To waiting here at home – a lifer's sentence.

Our crowd was groping in an alley
Through carnivals of vaseline, of leather.
One old boy would cry and we grew tired.
(We had to love them so much less than money.)
But even so they needed it:

The reddened room and in the driver's seat
A girl, whose husband beat her for a joke.
The body's ludicrous. We tried for style,
Until they ran me down this cul-de-sac
In dressing-gown, a PC at each side,

And only were not secretive or vile, enough.

## Déjeuner sur l'herbe

Mackenzie's shirtless,
Kneeling on rubbery
Grass to cadge some Thunderbird
Off Dougie, a novice
In translating the
Unenunciated word.

Mac's presided years
Over the crisp wrappers
Of a bachelors' picnic
On the flattened park verge,
Lacing his liquid
Takeaways with rhetoric;

This time passing out
Calm and cold, as the hunched
Accelerating homebound
Crowd ward off a hand-out
Of rain, eyes evading
The blessed body on the ground,

And the confrères, pissed-
On though they will be, wait
Until a man's comatose,
Breathing a bourn of mist,
Before they ransack
Wallet, carrier bag, clothes.

– Given what a round
Costs, merely practical:
Wheels within wheels, Dougie burrs,
*Wills within wills* it sounds
The way he says it,
As the three of them disperse.

## *from* A North London Planetary System

SATURN *at Hornsey Road*

Mr Saturn is wanted on the telephone.
There is a number for the other business
In the car or – if urgent – with the mistress,
Or he may be on his portable at the Ouzo café.

When there is a rush on; when there are orders
For the summer frocks, and aching eyes
And shoulders, the women may be comforted
On the rounds of the machines

By his casual icon, who – alert-breasted
Under a lush fountain streaming,
A Titaness from a magazine – surveys them
Fondly, as his light-tempered foreman.

Forgive us the furthest radiant of sorrow,
Where the child was last seen and the
Occasional evil circulates, frozen;
The time she can never make up
From that mania or this despair:
The woman who loses her children
To care, or the murdering lover.
Look, how the actor moves but the act
Disseminates, a grey sift raining
On us; have mercy: the hands that
Are raised bear the scars on each arm.

He's been a hand
On every sea,
   Navvied in ports.
The gulls winter
   Down the estuary.
He stumps the inland course
   Of hostels and DSS,
Missing the dawns
   And the absence of people,
His uphill walk
   Too stiff for pity;
His wants shrunk
   To an infallible kit.

# Fortuna

Of the countries, no one had their pick:
They lugged their bundles to the dock,
And sailed at night as if by magic.

Inland, a label flickered on a tree
In every plot. They heaped up turf
With an obstinate energy,

Plied against the sudden gun,
Or the slow march between warders
For what they'd never done.

## Success

The bride fled for cover, in her cheap dress.
The groom kept walking, nearly eight feet tall,
And thin and mean from lack of tenderness.

I waited for my friends in the great hall,
When Peter Lorre came in with the groom.
Their plans betrayed no tenderness, at all.

I hid until a gendarme, fingering a knife,
Said you're not the one we're after, after all.
Down the seven landings I went running for my life,

Found an open door, a room of bric-à-brac:
Crisp antimacassars, needle-filled housewife,
Brass baby boots and Monarchs in shellac.

I'm safe, although embarrassed to impose.
The woman, Pat, pretends she doesn't mind.
She's a sometime star in Royal Variety Shows,

Does a few soaps, a little music hall.
I won't go out. I feel it, and she knows:
Outside there is no tenderness at all.

## *from* Memo to Auden

Do you recall the teashop on the Broad?
You'd agreed to sit there daily
At four o'clock and dawdle, bored,
A big cat, for an exhibition fee:
Available for metric consultation
To any undergrad with nerve, or vision.

Gaping there, I lost an opportunity.
In fact I spilled Darjeeling on your shoe
(Smart Oxford brogue) and nearly missed
Watching the Jo'burg tourist corner you.
He brought a semaphoric forearm down
To shake your hand, quite heedless of your frown,

Luminous with praise,
And bombast and italicised exclaiming.
Your work had meant a lot to him, especially
That famous poem I'd re-offend by naming –
No gavel-wielding judge has ever rapped it
So sharply as Your Honour did: 'I scrapped it.'

Now to the old gnawed bone, that poetry
Makes nothing happen, the report
Of someone flatly sidelined by a war,
Who feels embarrassed holding down the fort –
Unheroically and not from duty –
Of common intellect and beauty.

The worst horrors can't be quantified,
Can't be healed, denied, forgot,
But implicit in the name of peace
Are its varied fruits, that rot
Under a swastika; its vines that die
Tied to the paling of a lie.

What is the alternative to art?
Religion of guns, guns of religion.
You know all this. You said it well,
But you have a grumpy disposition,
So I'm repeating, like an awkward kid,
What you tell us, Dad, ain't what you did.

In the careful mornings of the art
Over tonic cuppas in the lav,
Not to speak of sweaty collaboration
With Isherwood, Kallman, Britten, Strav,
You didn't do it for the bread alone:
Poets have to charm their bread from stone.

You didn't do it for the pick-up trade:
Most were arty foreigners, not rough.
You liked a wholesome share of fame
But found the poet tag absurd enough
When talking with commercial sorts on trains.
Other professions call for verve and brains,

But you chose this one. Why?
Words are saucy, difficult but willing.
You could play boss and close the study door.
But there was another end, as thrilling
When the scholar's breath went sour:
Coaxing lines from beauty gave her power,

And this was the Holy: an act of love
To damn the bunker, damn the bomb
And celebrate the individual life
Of myriad relations, from a room
Where the isolate voice is listened to
Through all its range, by such as you.

Let the victims, and their helpers,
And the guilty rest there for a time.
Let there be a commonality of good,
Gardens, architecture, rhyme,
That we betray by happenstance,
Forgiving airs to make us dance.

P.S. Myself I have too much to learn
Of voice and sense. You used this metre,
Don Juan too, but in our day
It's not exactly a world-beater.
Still, 'subtle' can mean convoluted
And for our little chat, it suited.